Paris rooftops

The Eiffel Tower

Notre-Dame Cathedral

Pont Alexandre III

The Louvre

Musée d'Orsay

Sainte-Chapelle

Tour de France on the Champs-Élysées with the Arc de Triomphe in view

The Métro

The Palais-Royal

Window-box geraniums

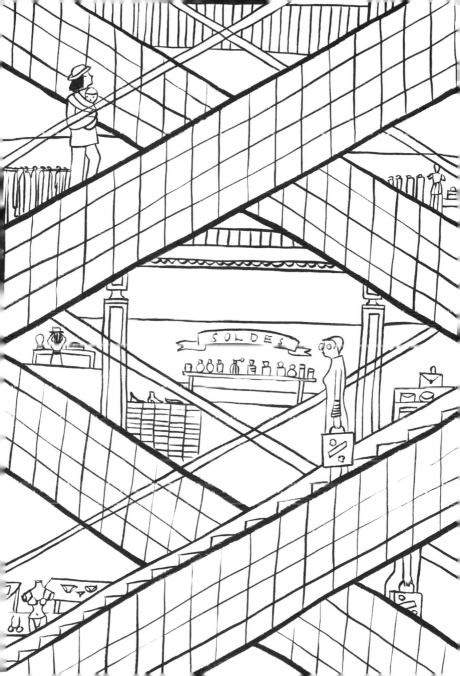

Le Bon Marché

A boulangerie

Tuileries Garden

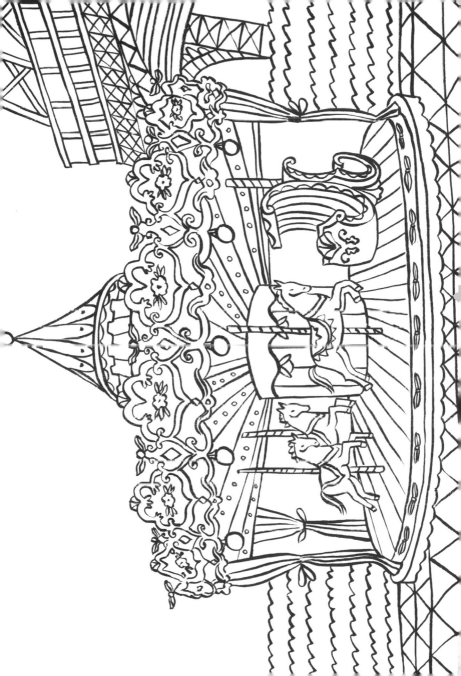

A carousel at the Champs de Mars

A puppet show in the park

Le Marais

Place des Vosges

SAUCISSON

BAGUETTE

A French picnic

A café in the Latin Quarter

A patisserie

Booksellers along the Seine

Boisserie

Flea-market treasures

Montmartre